First Science

Keep it Afloat!

© 1993 Watts Books

First Published in Great Britain
in 1993 by
Watts Books
96 Leonard Street
London
EC2A 4RH

Franklin Watts Australia
14 Mars Road
Lane Cove
NSW 2066

Editorial planning: Serpentine Editorial
Scientific consultant: Dr J.J.M.Rowe

Designed by The R & B Partnership
Illustrator: David Anstey
Photographer: Peter Millard

Additional photographs:
Chris Fairclough Colour Library 10,12;
ZEFA 11, 14, 20, 22, 29, 30 (top), 31 (top);
G I Bernard/NHPA 30 (bottom).

UK ISBN: 0 7496 1087 5
A CIP catalogue record for this book is
available from the British Library

10 9 8 7 6 5 4 3 2 1

Printed in Malaysia

Keep it Afloat!

Julian Rowe
and Molly Perham

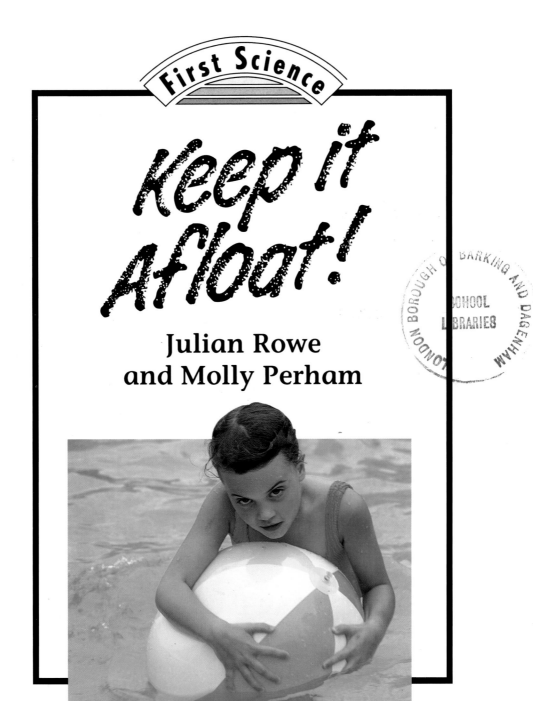

WATTS BOOKS

London • New York • Sydney

Contents

SAFETY WARNING

Activities marked with this symbol require the presence and help of an adult. Plastic should always be used instead of glass. Take special care near water.

Floaters and sinkers

This girl is sailing her boat on the pool.
It floats on the water.
A puff of wind fills
the sail and takes
the boat to the
other side.

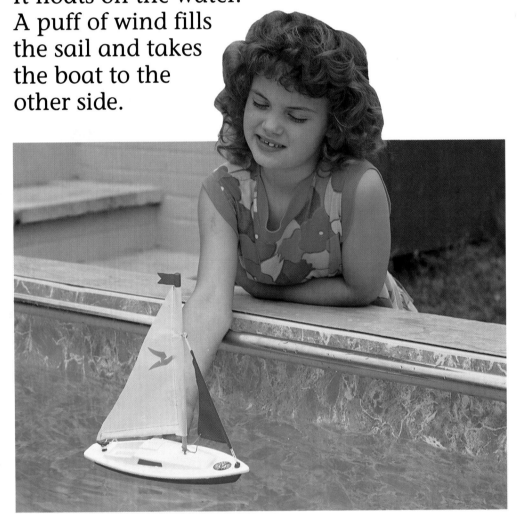

Have you ever thrown a pebble into a pool?
It sinks straight to the bottom.
All you see is a circle of ripples
on the surface of the pool.

Test it out

This boy is collecting all kinds of things to test. Some of them are natural objects such as a lemon, shells, a cork and a fir-cone. Others are household objects.

Which things float and which sink? How can you find out?

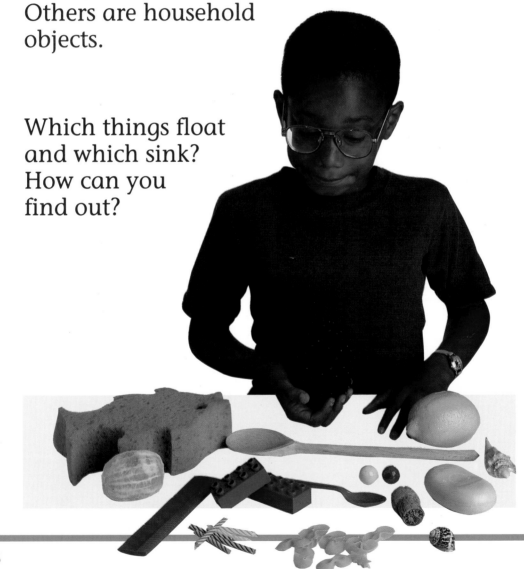

You can use a plastic fish tank or large bowl to test things. See how the marbles and the shells have sunk to the bottom. Which things are floating on the top?

The lemon floats because the peel contains tiny pockets of air. Why does the peeled lemon sink?

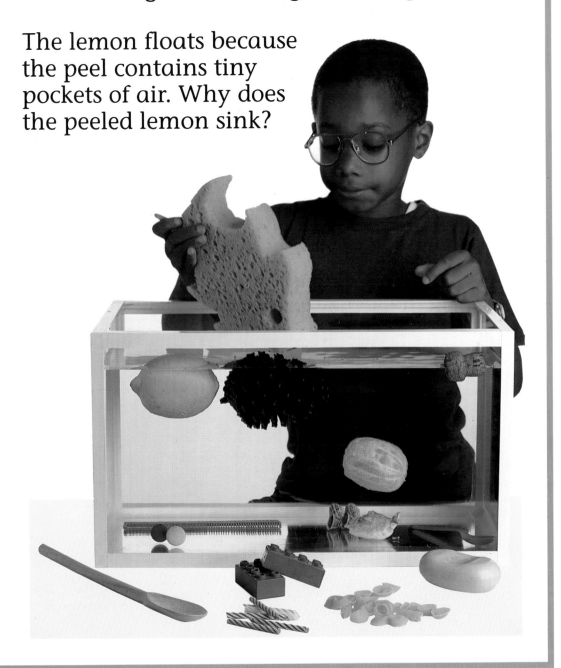

Boats afloat

Inside the hull of a sailing dinghy there
are hollow spaces filled with air.
These stop the dinghy sinking if
it is blown over, or capsizes.

A giant passenger liner is very heavy.
It weighs as much as a big building.

But it floats because, like the dinghy,
its hull is hollow and contains air.

Cargo ships

This ship carries thousands of tonnes of cargo. The heavy containers are carefully loaded so that the boat does not tip over and sink.

Make a cargo ship

Find some kitchen
foil, a pair of scissors
and some small
pebbles.

Cut a piece of foil the size of this page.
Bend up the edges on each side.

Fold the corners so
that water cannot
get in.

Float your boat in
a bucket full of water.
Now try loading it
with pebbles.
What happens if you
put them all in
one corner?

13

water pushes back

Have you ever paddled an inflatable boat? Why do you think it floats so easily in the water?

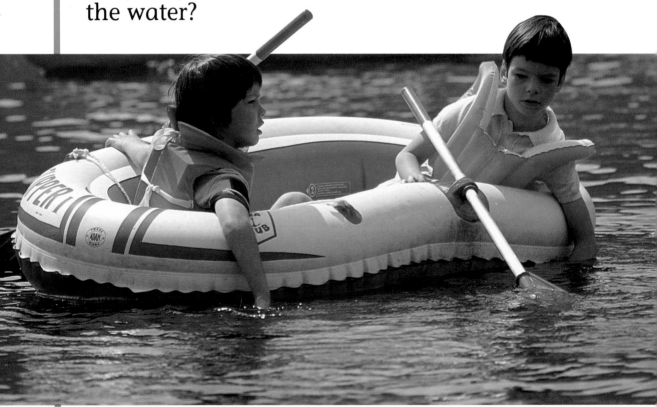

When you push the paddle through the water, can you feel the water pushing back?

This big ball is full of air. It floats right on top of the water. If you try to sink it, you can feel the water pushing back.

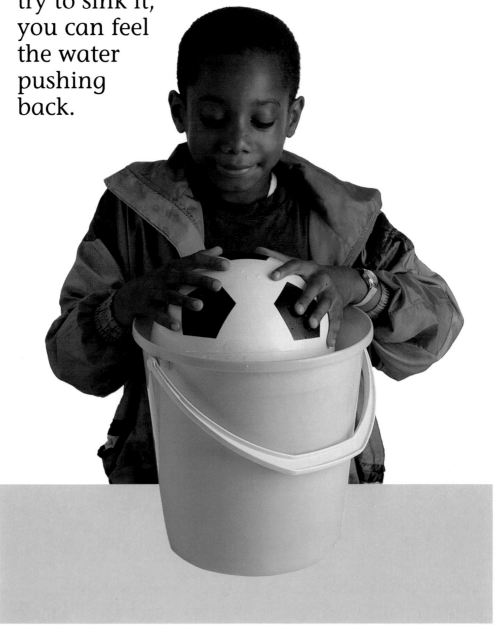

Learning to swim

Have you ever played with a beach
ball in the water?

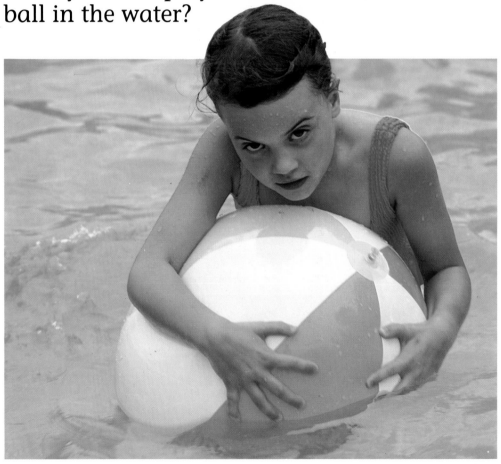

If you hold on to the ball, it will
keep you afloat, or buoyant.

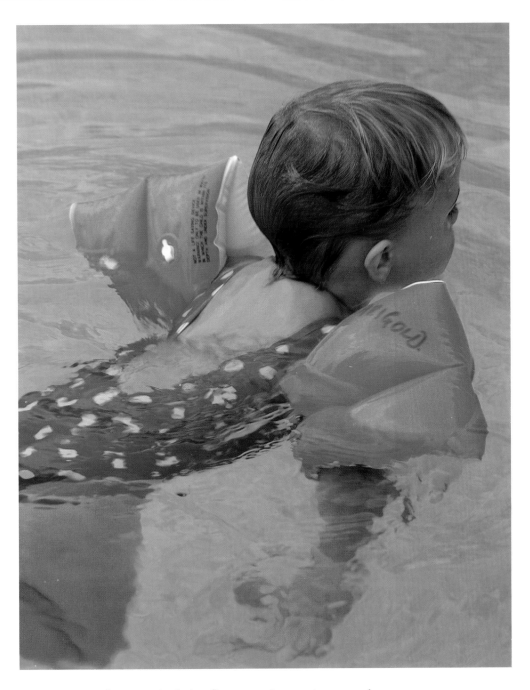

This girl is learning to swim.
Her armbands are full of air.
They are called buoyancy aids.

Under the water

Plants that live under the water have pockets of air inside them. These keep the plants floating in the water.

Fish have their own buoyancy aid, called a swim bladder, inside their bodies.
They can control the amount of air in the swim bladder. This allows them to float higher or lower in the water.

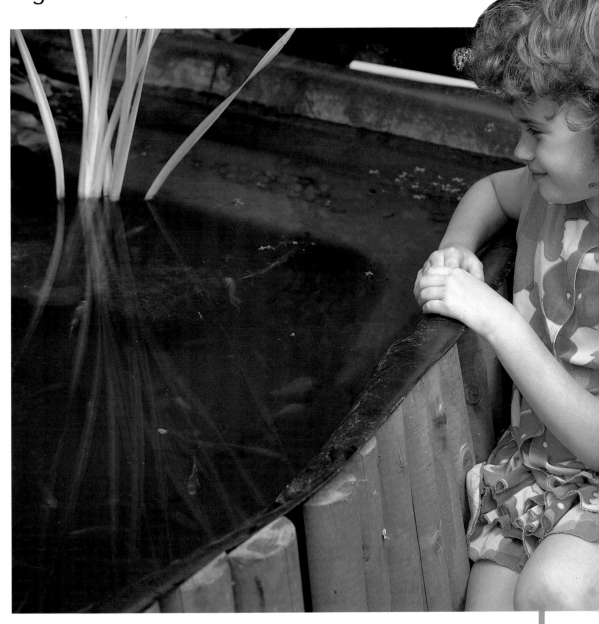

Submarines

A submarine rises up and sinks down in the water like a fish.

When it dives, air is pumped out of its buoyancy tanks and water comes in. When the water is blown out, the submarine rises.

Make a submarine

Sharp tool

Find a plastic bottle, a piece of plastic tubing and some plasticine.

Make a hole in the bottom of the bottle. Cover it with plasticine.

Make a hole in the cap. Push the piece of plastic tubing through it.

Fill the bottle with water. Screw the cap back on.

Put your submarine under water in a large bowl or tank. Remove the plasticine.

Now blow down the tube and watch your submarine rise to the surface.

Lighter than water

Some things float because they are lighter than water. Ice is lighter than water.

Huge icebergs float in the seas around the North Pole.

Make an iceberg

Find an empty yoghurt pot. Fill it with water and put it in the freezer.

When the water has frozen, hold the yoghurt pot under a running tap until the ice inside loosens. Take out the block of ice.

Put your iceberg in a bowl of water. How much is under the water?

Oil and water

Oil is lighter than water.
It spreads out on the
surface of the water.
When it rains, you can
see oily patterns in
puddles on the street.

If a tanker spills some oil at sea, the oil
spreads far and wide.
It does not mix with the water.

White spirit

Make oily pictures

Find some oil paints, white spirit, an oven tray, some thick paper and an old fork.

Fill the tray with water, and add a spoonful of white spirit.

Put some drops of oil paint onto the water.

Stir the colours around with the fork to make a pattern.

Carefully lay the piece of paper flat on the water.
Lift the paper quickly and let the water drip off. Pin your picture up to dry.

Soapy water

Oil mixes with water if detergent is added. These children are washing greasy plates using a detergent.

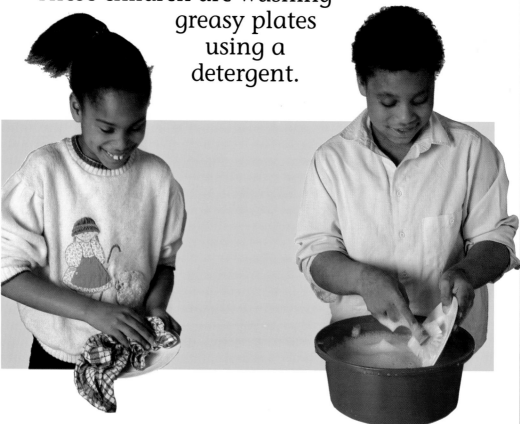

When seabirds swim into oily water, the oil sticks to their feathers. The oil can be removed with a detergent, which is then washed away.

Mixing oil and water

Find a clean empty bottle with a screw cap, some washing-up liquid and some cooking oil.

Put some oil in the bottle.

Half fill the bottle with water. See how the oil rises to the top.

Add a few drops of washing-up liquid.

Now screw the cap onto the bottle and give it a good shake. What has happened to the oil?

Floating on air

Just as some liquids are lighter than water, some gases are lighter than air. The boy is holding balloons filled with helium gas. Helium is lighter than air, so the balloons float.

Hot-air balloons float because the warm air inside them is lighter than the cold air outside.

Think about... floating

Ducks spend most of their day floating on water. The quills of their feathers are hollow and contain air.

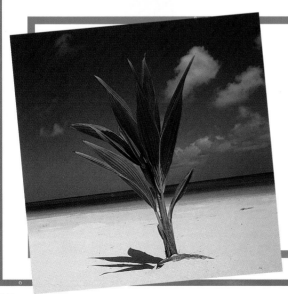

Giant coconuts float for hundreds of miles from one island to another in the Pacific Ocean. These seeds then grow into new trees.

What is the easiest way to move heavy logs?
In Canada great rafts of logs are pulled by
tug-boat to the sawmill.

Have you ever put a
message in a bottle?
If you throw it into
the ocean, it could
float all the way to
another country.

INDEX